For You
A Collection of Love Poems

by Keri Brye

PITTSBURGH, PENNSYLVANIA 15222

ISBN: 978-1-4349-9132-4
Library of Congress Control Number: 2008925167

Printed in the United States of America

First Printing

For information or to order additional books, please write:
RoseDog Books
701 Smithfield St.
Third Floor
Pittsburgh, PA 15222
U.S.A.
1-800-834-1803
www.rosedogbookstore.com

Acknowlegements

Every accomplishment is achieved with support. I couldn't have accomplished this book without the support of my family. Thank you very much, everyone, for believing in me.

Thank God, all things are possible through belief in him.

"...all things are possible to him that believeth," **Mark 9:23.**

My family: Mom, thanks for always reminding me that "life is what you make it," Kernon, my husband for accepting "all" of me, Dad, Step-dad, Larry, Grandma Bertha, for your home-made biscuits and syrup and prayer clothes; the nourishment and spiritual support for this book, Grandma Young, Grandpa Young, my aunts Melody, Patricia, Linda, Darnetta, Carol, and Diane, uncles Vincent, for his support with college, James, Tadarel, Tony, and Edgar. To all my cousins and friends, thank you for making me smile, and a special thanks to my daughter, Paris for brightening my life.

To Stephanie,

Best Wishes

Keri Brye

Contents

In Love

Meant to be 1
Falling 3
A Promise 5
Marry Me 7
Synonym for Love 9
Some Kind of Wonderful 11
Hope 14
I Just Know 16
He Is 18

Deeper in Love

Making Love 19
A Kiss 20
Because of Love 21
You Are 23
A Reminder 24
Dre 25
Walking With Love 27
The Treasure 30
The One 32

Deep in Love

Remember When 33
The Medicine 35
A Smile like Yours 37
Thinking of You 39
Thank You 40
I Appreciate You 41
The Meaning of an Anniversary 42
Kernon's Sun 44

Wedding Vows

No mistakes 45
Why I'm Here 47
Always 48

Sexy Suggestions

Sexy Suggestions 49

Ways to Propose

Proposal Ideas 51

Short Stories

Meant to Be 53
The Blessing...58

Preface

I was always a hopeless romantic. I have been writing poetry since I was about eight years old, and my poems matured with me. Once in high school, my poems were mainly centered on love and romance. I was often the one to whom friends would confide to receive my romantic ideas and suggestions. Nothing changed when I went to college. I continued writing poems, and my new friends would also confide in me for romantic suggestions.

Then something changed. A friend asked me for a great idea for proposing to someone, and I gave them a few suggestions,for which they were willing to pay me. That friend told other people, who began coming to me for suggestions and ideas on how to propose or just a simple romantic evening. I then began making cards, writing romantic letters, poems, and even wedding vows for couples. One day another friend saw my spiral binder containing over 250 poems and said, "Why won't you get those published?" I thought about it but was always too busy to sit and do something about it. Then after my fairy tale-themed wedding, many people came to me and complimented me on my vows and the story that was read during the ceremony. They asked me where I had found the story and who made up my vows. When I told them that I did, they were stunned. Then the same suggestion was given to me for the second time in my life. "Girl, you should write a book. You are good at romantic ideas. People could use those suggestions." I began to think about it again, but the task of being a new mom, wife, and full- time teacher became too busy for me.

I would recite some of my poems to my husband and make cards using the poems. Then one day, after reciting a poem, my husband asked, "Keri, when are you going to publish that stuff? Your poems are really good." So I pulled out my mom's laptop and began to fill the blank screen. I have over 250 poems but have selected only my favorite love poems for this book because the subject of love is what I'm good at.

For your pleasure, here is a copy of the vows and the fairy tale story that was recited at my wedding. Enjoy!

• • •

Our Fairytale

Once upon a time, before they were born, a boy and girl so madly in love created a plan so they would recognize each other on earth.

This was the plan:

They would share the same lucky number, seven, for it would connect them in many ways. They would be born for one another, sharing birth dates in the same month, September and year, 1978 when combined equals seven. However, he would set out on his journey first on September 2, to ensure the world was safe for his future wife. She would soon follow on September 12.

Their names,(Kernon and Keri would begin with the root word "Ker," which means "to grow," for they were destined to grow together. She alone would bare a name which comes from the name of two ancient rivers (a symbol of her and him) and it would mean "to love."

They met for the first time on earth in kindergarten class and instantly bonded. They enjoyed playing in the sandbox and the class's playhouse, where they acted the roles of husband and wife, unaware these would be their future titles. The next eighteen years through elementary, middle, and high school were spent secretly admiring each other, staring at each other, uttering awkward hellos and giving friendly hugs. One day at an event swarming with thousands of people, they ran into each other and the flame rekindled. They were engaged on Valentine's Day 2004, had a beautiful baby girl, Paris ten months later and planned to unite in holy matrimony the following year. Here they are today, in the spirit of the magic that bought them together, uniting for the beginning of their happily ever after.

The Beginning

•   •   •

Vows

Husband's vows:
Keri Trenisha Young, I love you very much. You are a precious flower to me. You light up my life even on the darkest day. There are so many things that are not promised throughout life, but there is one thing that I can promise you....Forever. I promise to:
Fully commit myself to you and always be your best friend.
Only love you and no one else.
Respect every wish that you ask of me.
Enjoy every minute of my life with you.
Visualize your beautiful face even when you are away from me.
Express my thoughts and feelings to you.
Remain by your side through sickness, health, richer or poorer, til death do us part.

My vows:
Kernon, I've waited on this moment my entire life and at this very moment, I know that all of my prayers have been answered and all of my dreams have come true.
So I am fully prepared to fully commit myself to you.
Through the demands of the present and the uncertainties of the future, I promise to be faithful, open, and honest with you and to love and support you in all of your endeavors. I promise to lift you when you're down, laugh with you,

cry with you, grow with you, and pray with you; through good and bad times, for storms always pass. When you are sick, I will nurse you back to health. For richer or poorer, for love itself is rich. Most importantly, I promise you infinite love, for it is pure and constant. For the rest of my natural life, I will love, honor, cherish, and respect you.

I fully commit myself to you in the name of the Father, who lead me to you and who will light the paths of our future, in the name of the Holy Spirit, for this is a holy union and in the name of the Son, for he is *love*.

Meant to Be

We will meet one day.

Everything about us will have…

One rhythm.

My name will be hidden in his

And his in mine.

Our hearts will share

The same beat.

We will speak

One voice.

We will share

One thought.

We will smell

One respect.

We will taste

One truth.

We will hear

One inner truth.

Our feet will walk

One path.

When we meet outside our dream,

We will walk that path

Together.

Like a jigsaw puzzle,

We will fit.

I will be the fit

Of his missing piece.

A combination of his lucky numbers

Will equal mine.

A dream of seven years

Will then have a face,

A face recognizable from day

One.

And our hands will have

Matching life lines

For we were meant to share a life

Together.

Falling

I'm at the top of a high building

Not knowing what to do.

Thinking, should I stay aboard safety

Or listen to you?

There's a structure up there

And I'm holding on tight.

I'm debating on letting go

Or continuing to fight.

A mental battle

Stay and be protected

Or

Fall and risk being neglected?

I hold on to the structure.

My adrenaline pumps.

I'm scared!

But I prepare to jump.

You lift my hands from the structure

So I'd let go.

I'm falling now, miles per second

But it feels so slow.

I thought I'd be hurting,

But I feel secure.

I've dreamed of this fall my entire life,

This time, I'm sure.

I'm glad you set me free.

I'm enjoying the leap.

Don't stop me now.

I'm falling...

In love.

A Promise

I know you don't make promises

For you know not what the future holds.

You know promises are just as easily broken

As they are spoken.

Choosing to break yours or having yours broken.

Times are different, times are hard

Especially with two hearts to guard.

We live in a imperfect world

And we are not perfect people;

But perfect for each other.

We're going to stumble,

We are going to fall.

If we believe in each other

We will rise above it all.

Faith will keep us moving.

Faith is something we should keep

We must.

As long as it is in love that

We trust.

As we embrace,

As we kiss,

We can expect a future

For love is a promise.

Marry Me

No one can equal up to you.

No one can compare to things you do.

You fill each day with excitement,

Always with something new.

The bad days are even good.

The worst ones are too.

Anything dark,

Will brighten next to you.

No one talks like you

Or smiles the way you do.

No one listens like you listen

When I bring problems to you.

No one is as inspiring as you

Or love passionate like you love.

No one has the glow in their eyes

Or innocence of a dove.

No one has ever meant what they said

Or took action upon their words.

You speak with value only

And actions follow each word.

You fill each day with delight,

Making the next worth looking forward to.

I want to know if you'd marry me

Because I want to marry you.

Synonym for Love

I've never had to say it

Because this thing he was.

Deleting all of the antonyms

My synonym for love.

It was never blind to me,

I saw all that he was made of.

Not another simile,

My synonym for love.

I can't ask for more,

When I have it all.

No simile, but metaphor

My synonym for love.

Not a mere personification

Action speaks louder than words.

Reality overpowers imagination

My synonym for love.

All is pure.

A lively fairytale.

Something others wish to lure

My synonym for love.

I've never had to wish for it,

He's more than it is made of.

I don't have to crave it

My synonym for love.

Some Kind of Wonderful

May I ask who it is

That you may be?

Do you know what it is

That you do to me?

Whoever it is

That you are,

You must be from

A distant star.

- Because of the things,

That you made me feel.

However, they cannot

Be for real.

When staring into each

Other's eyes we soar

To a place man's heart

Has never been before:

Above the clouds,

Above earth's sky

Too busy to stop

And ask you why.

Whenever we kiss,

I forget my name.

And my present and future

Suddenly change.

Because I've been to

A magic place,

More honest than truth

In more harmony than grace.

Maybe you are another

Dimension of supreme.

Maybe you crept into reality

Out of a desired dream,

Where you were to moon

Brightening my darkest hours

And becoming the sun,

To dry my showers.

You are the clouds,

On which I float

On a heavenly high

Of blissful gloat.

Whoever it is

That you may be,

You've brought many

Great joys to me.

Whether you be from near

Or from afar

You are some kind of wonderful

That's what you are.

Hope

I've been gone for a long time.

I was abducted by a dark cloud

That constantly rained on me.

The rain seeped through my pores

And soaked my soul

With sadness.

Then you came.

I was abducted by Hope.

You constantly shine sun rays on me.

The rays seeped through my pores

And dried out my soul,

Brightening my heart.

Then the storm came

And tried to flood out your hope.

Lightning struck my heart

And seeped through my pores,

Shocking my soul

And scattering my heart.

Then you showed me proof

That we are stronger than any storm.

With just one look in my eyes,

Hope's rays out-shined the storm

And replaced my heart's pieces;

I'm whole.

I Just Know

Sometimes, when you look for something

You look over it.

Sometimes, when you stop looking,

It finds you.

But how will you know

You've looked over it?

How will you know

To stop looking?

How will you know

It's discovered you?

I didn't know

Then

I do know

Now.

I don't know how,

But I do know

That I know.

I know also

To let feelings show,

Not to hide them inside.

Let them glow.

Show them with pride,

Let the world know.

Water them each day,

With love,

Let them grow.

I know that what we feel will grow.

I don't know how,

But I just know.

He Is

Jaunty is his personality.

Eccentric is the type he is.

Sincere to me everyday,

Splendid in every way;

Eloquent.

Warmhearted is his heart.

Affectionate is his mind.

Laborious person he is to understand;

Darling all the time.

Radiant is his smile,

Opiate is his eyes,

Natural is the way he is all of the time.

Making Love

I boiled a bag of strength,

Added a pound of honesty,

Two bags of faith,

A can of respect,

A dozen kisses,

A bottle of hugs,

An ounce of caressing,

And a package of love.

I put it in a bowl

And mixed it together.

As soon as I was ready

To put it in the oven,

I thought, damn....

How can I make love,

Without the other package of loving?

A Kiss

It is a song more pleasurable than any.

A song many love to hear,

A song with a flowing harmony

The sweetest music to my ear.

A song that whispers softly.

A song that acts as it sings.

A song that expresses its emotions

The sweetest song anyone can sing.

A song that's relaxing.

It puts the mind at ease.

It means more than words.

It's guaranteed to please.

A song that never ends.

A song that never lies.

A song unfilled with sin.

Its notes are higher than the skies.

A kiss.

Because of Love

The touch of your hands

Soothes every woman's desire.

Your presence fills every woman's needs.

Your charm soothes women uncontrollably.

You have a reputation to sweep women off the ground.

Women swoon because you have the best looks in town

And have never been known to let any woman down.

You've done this to every woman.

All except me.

One day I was alone,

I saw you pass by

You came on to me strong.

I decided to give you a try.

True, your talk was smooth,

True, your moves were fly.

But they were not enough for me to buy.

Maybe enough for other women,

All except me.

My love's extraordinary.

His hands soothe my desire

And when touched my soul blazed afire.

His presence fills my every need

And fills my soul with enough love to bleed.

His charm pleases me uncontrollably

It puts me in a trance.

The fires in my soul explode and dance.

His looks may not be the best in town

But enough to sweep me off the ground.

It still has not let me down.

Everything he does,

Seems extraordinary to me,

Because of love I feel this way,

Because of love,

I'm pleased.

You Are

You are a beautiful rose,

Soft and fluffy about the rim.

As beautiful as the sun that shines,

As warm as this heart of mine.

My heart with pleasure fills

And blows like wind among the hills.

You make my soul fill with please

You put my mind forever at ease.

Floating like the waves in the seas

In hot weather feeling a cool breeze,

You are.

A Reminder

Just a reminder,

I was thinking of you

And all of the wonderful things you do.

Just to assure you my feelings are true.

I love you I really do.

Passion fills me when thinking of you

And how your words are proven true.

Just appreciation for being by my side,

For lifting me up and giving me pride.

Just a reminder that my love is real.

For you it's real, for you it's real.

Just a reminder you're on my mind

Just a reminder we're two of a kind.

Let me remind you past loves are through

And my love for you is true.

You stick to my heart like glue, like glue.

My love for you is true, true, true.

Dre

_I have a friend whose name is Dre.

He is very special and dear to me.

I see these things in remembrance of Dre:

The Sun.

Dre brightens me up like a summer's day.

His face sways back and forth in my mind.

He whispers words with his heart

And speaks to me with unspoken words.

The Stars

Dre shines like the stars.

He gives me confidence higher than trees,

Bringing only pleasant thoughts to my mind,

Sacredly keeping the inner part of me.

Beauty.

Beautiful like a rose from head to foot.

He is wise, never weakened or unshuttered in the root.

His stem rises to face the sun in the morning's sky.

He is ignorant to distress, he washes it aside.

His memory's brighter than the rays of the sun

That each day shines the same.

Dre; the days when night never came.

As night subsides to a brand new day,

I'll see these things in remembrance of Dre,

Dre is love.

walking with Love

Have you ever experienced love?

Do you even know the meaning of?

Come walk with me, for I am love,

Let me show you what I am made of.

Let's walk down my gentle streets,

While in my language I will speak.

Let me hold your hand and guide you through,

And show you the meaning of the words"I do."

Come look through my eyes and see

All of the goodness inside of me.

Let me assure you, there's nothing to be afraid of,

Let me show you what I am made of.

Hearts are broken, but not caused by me.

But caused by my brother, Unfaithfully.

Pain occurs often, but it's not something I do.

If you suffer pain, you've met my sister, Untrue.

I am gentle, sweet, and also kind.

I am what eases a frustrated mind.

I lay your head down upon my breast,

Until you can peacefully rest.

I'm the motivator,

Not the procrastinator.

I am Forever,
Not, "See You Later."

I am a confident incentive

Not the non-complementive.

Joy is the only reason I make you cry

Not because of a sad goodbye.

For it is I,

For it is I.

Walk with me and live to love,

Walk with me and love til die.

Come with me and forever smile,

Come with me, it's worth your while.

Now can you see all the things inside

That loves without dominance and knocks out pride.

Come with me and feel like you should.

Come with me and love for good.

Spend my time, make your dreams come alive.

One day in reality, in love is 365.

See with my eyes, the eyes of love.

Touch with my hands, as gentle as a dove.

Walk with my feet and almost glide.

Taste my fruit, now pure inside.

You will never know my brother Unfaithfully,

Or my sister Untrue.

For I've filled you with forever

And the meaning of I do.

Stand at attention my soldier,

The war has passed us by.

Live to love, walk with Forever.

Love til die, apart thee never.

The Treasure

Since I first came to be

I felt as if I were incomplete

I searched for satisfaction for the empty space

But nothing could fill that barren place

I thought I'd be content with silver or gold

But the wholeness would not unfold

I thought the answer was money or success

I pushed myself to be the best

I was very accomplished but wanted more

I never knew exactly what I was searching for

I discovered that searching would not find

What was there all the time

The treasure that I was looking for

Wasn't silver or gold, but something more

It isn't buried underneath the ground

When discovered it's sure to astound

Put away your shovel; no need to dig

For something greater than great, bigger than big

It is so much bigger than yourself

Sure to earn you a greater wealth

It's not money or success

Of anything, it is the best

It's not a diamond or a pearl

But the greatest treasure in the world

It's not the silver or the gold

Instead it's love that's made me whole

I've searched the world over to find

God's treasure; one of a kind

It took some time for me to see

God made this treasure just for me

I've searched for this treasure; one of kind

I found treasure and this one's mine.

The One

Karat of brown, with a value of gold

Amulet of seduction I desire to unfold.

Raging hands of fire,

Labyrinth of desire.

Alluring voice that thrills

Leaving my body with chills

Lavishing and benevolent

Eloquent.

Noble.

Remember when

While looking through that window there,

I see the wind and you kissing my hair,

And making the satin sheets massage our skin.

While your heart beat massages me within.

Your eyes define me while staring in mine.

Mine meet yours back and love they find.

As your tongue caresses mine,

Your fingers slowly explore my spine.

With your fingers, you comb my hair.

Your tongue lotions me everywhere.

Becoming human burritos wrapped in sheets,

We mix our sauces in our heat.

Our bodies steam as we scream like kettles.

We pant, we caress, we fondle and meddle.

We boil over and everything ends.

We cool down and remember when.

The many nights and many days.

We'd love each other many ways.

While lying side by side we dream,

Of how long ago these days seem.

Sunlight came and ended the night,

Awakening us with its light,

That peeped in through our door.

We began a sequel of the night before.

The Medicine

His lab jacket was caramel.

His badge read "Dr. More."

With each step he cast a spell

When walking into the door.

When he put on his glove my heart fired,

In fear of the steel-like erection.

Like defrosting food I perspired

Preparing for the injection.

You will barely feel this,

In those words the truth and lie united.

He grabbed my arm for the steel kiss

And I tried not to fight it.

His thick alcohol prep licked my skin

With each stroke up and down.

Pretending to be okay within,

Trying to calm myself down.

Aiming his needle for my vein

It grazed the surface of my skin.

Ready for the blissful pain,

Surprisingly, it didn't go in.

Finally, the warm steel went in.

Making my arm a little sore,

Deeper and deeper he injected it in

And in repetition, I read his name, Dr. More.

A Smile Like Yours

A smile that shines and brightens the night

Making my world seem perfectly right.

Twinkling like little diamond stars

Taking my mind away; very far.

Just like a star high in the sky,

A little diamond in my life.

Beaming like the sun on a feverish day,

Brings a smile to my face.

Unlike anything I've ever known

A set of white fluorescent glows.

Each morning I see the sun create another day,

But most faces I see rarely smile that way.

I've seen sun rays outline the clouds

But never a smile speaking each language aloud.

I've seen the sun set to begin the night,

But never a smile like the moonlight.

I've seen many rainbows after each rain,

But never a smile that can ease pain.

I've seen the moon highlight the sea

But never a smile bright enough to brighten me.

I've seen feather-like waves wash along shores

But never a smile as bright as yours.

Thinking of You

Wherever I am,

Whatever I do,

You can count on me

Thinking of you.

Thank You

I just wanted to say thank you.

For all the things that you do.

For the times I'm sad,

You pull me through.

When I'm down,

You lift me up.

Bringing me through

Times that are rough.

Taking me out of the night

Bringing me into the light.

Thank you for caring and being my friend

Thank you for lending a helping hand.

Thank you, thank you

To the one that I adore.

Thank you,

Each day I love you more.

I Appreciate You

I appreciate

Each time you've kissed me

And each time you've said you've missed me.

I appreciate

Your sensitive side

Buried underneath your foolish pride.

I appreciate

You coming around,

Lifting me up me when I feel down.

I appreciate

You putting up with me.

I know how sometimes that can be.

I know that you don't think I do,

But with deepest sincerity,

I appreciate you.

The Meaning of an Anniversary

What does it really means to me

To have an anniversary?

It's not just another date of a year

To exchange gifts and toast or cheer.

It's a day to celebrate the love in our hearts

To celebrate our unity and thank God we aren't apart.

To think back on rough times and when green bills were few

We look at each other and say, "We made it through.

Through the rain and through the storms,

We fought together with no done harm.

It's a day to smile and cheer,

We're blessed to make it through another year.

Not one, not two, not three or four

We fought this long, let's fight for more.

Thank God, Who sits above

For enabling us to celebrate this year of love.

Thank God, who awoke you this anniversary morn,

To celebrate the day our love was born.

Kernon's Sun
Dedicated to my loving husband

It's an infinite spring

Giving life to everything,

Never shining too dull or bright.

Giving temperatures of comfort and endless delight.

Never to set, but always rise,

The moon infinitely hibernates under his skies.

Time stands still and never unfolds

And his green is always gold

Celebrating life and growth has begun

Winter never comes under Kernon's Sun.

A boundless joy that shuns sorrow

And brings definite promises of tomorrow.

Sun kissed away tears, a new world begun,

Darkness never falls under Kernon's sun.

wedding vows

Before I decided on which set of wedding vows to recite to my husband on our wedding day, I wrote four and decided on one. These are the ones I composed for my wedding. If you are planning to marry, feel free to use these vows as your own. If you are already married, you can use them as poems for your spouse or if you plan to renew your vows. Enjoy!

Sample I:

NO MISTAKES

When God put me here,

A long time ago,

I did not know

Where I would go.

I did not know

Who I wanted to be.

I had to figure out

How to be me.

Then I found you.

Now, I know

Where it is

That I will go.

It was then

That I began to see,

Who it was

I wanted to be.

It was then,

I became complete

Now, I'm comfortable

Just being me.

I guess it's true that

Where the heart rests is home.

I know it is with you

That I belong.

I've been doubtful of many things,

But this is something I know.

I'm sure I belong with you,

Because God told me so.

Know that God leads me

Through each decision I make

He led me to you

And He makes no mistakes.

Sample II

WHY I'M HERE

I can't think of any other reason

God put me on this earth

Except for you.

I am a woman of God

And through his service.

I commit myself to you.

Sample III

ALWAYS

All gold doesn't glitter

But every diamond shines

I don't need you tailor made

Just to know you're mine

I'm only half;

Together we are one.

I wanted to be complete

I am now, you're the one.

You have my soul

You have my heart,

We're a unit, we'll be together

Even when we're apart.

Sexy Suggestions

We are always looking for ways to maintain the smoldering summer heat in the winter of the relationship. Before my husband I were married, we compiled a list of ideas so we would not get bored. We made a copy for use on rainy days. We never know when one of us will use an idea from the list to surprise each other. Of course, we are always adding to the list. Here is a list of things that my husband and I do to surprise each other. We learned from hearing other couples complain about doing the same things over again and getting bored with it. So we made this list to make sure we would always have something new to try with which to romance and surprise each other. We even included those things that we were not thrilled to try.

1. **Surprises!** Be original and creative and keep surprises coming.

2. **Role play** Pretend that you are just meeting each other and ask the stranger for a date.

3. **Games** Play romantic games with each other, whether board games or self invented ones.

4. **Weekends away** Creates an urge for spouse, call and talk erotically to spouse.

5. **In town Rendezvous**- Go rent a hotel suite and spend a few days there. It does not have to be a special occasion.

6. **Be Bold** Don't be afraid to do something wild and exciting. For example:

   a) Rent a limo for no other reason than to take a romantic tour of your hometown.

   b) Go for a horse and carriage ride.

   c) For your anniversary or birthday, Rent out a movie theater for you and your spouse and have a personalized message on the screen.

   d) Re-propose on any anniversary, changing the original approach.

   e) Plan a surprise getaway without your spouse's knowledge. Make sure all details are complete.

7. **Love Letters** Continue to write love letters occasionally.

8. **Intimate Alternatives** Find new ways to be intimate. Hold back on love making for a while and find other ways to reach sexual peaks. Example: caress, hold, or kiss until climax is reached. Be creative with tools for stimulation, example: Scarf rose, silk, pearls, etc.

9. **Continual Dating** Call spouse from work and pretend not to know each other. Ask spouse out on a date. Each time, change the approach and place. For example: come to spouse's job and ask for date, have spouse's closest friend ask for you.

10. **Competition** Have romantic competitions. Compete with each other for most romantic date. Take turns planning dates and each time try to do better than spouse's previous date. At the end of the date, reward the winner with a place of their choice or create your own idea.

11. **Candle light anything** Candlelight even the most common daily tasks. For example: conversations, dinner, picnics, bath, massage, movie.

12. **Jokes** Tell jokes, if you can invent erotic jokes. It creates both happiness and excitement for spouse.

13. **Walks** Go on long walks. Be sure to hold each other close and/or hold hands. Reminisce about old times or bring a new idea to light.

14. **Show interest** Continue to ask questions about spouse as if you just met him or her.

15. **Reminisce** Continue to reminisce about relationship.

16. **Flirt** Continue to flirt with your spouse. This helps keep the excitement going. The relationship will always feel new.

17. **Compliment** Give occasional compliments. This makes spouse feel confident and happy.

18. **Brainstorm** Continue to brainstorm new ideas to be added to the list this will keep ideas flowing in. Your list will grow and you will never run out of things to do.

Ways to Propose

Here is a list of suggested proposal ideas for friends who have asked for help. These are some of the ideas I gave to them.

Proposal Ideas

1. Ask spouse for date to favorite restaurant. Ask server for a "to go" box of Jell-O and have ring placed inside of the Jell-O. You can have date open the box at the restaurant or at a place of your choice.

2. Have a helicopter fly by with a message tagging along. Call your local helicopter renting agents for this.

3. Art gallery Consult with an artist of your choice and have him or her complete a picture just for this occasion of a wedding ring or a hand with a wedding ring being placed on it or something of your choice. Try and have them include it in an upcoming art exhibition. Take your spouse to the gallery for art exhibition.

4. Photograph collage Create a photograph collage in sequence so that the pictures tell a story when you flip the page. The last few photographs should consist of one being on your knees and the next of the engagement ring.

5. CD Compile a mixed CD with you and your companion's favorite songs. Record your voice asking, "Will you marry me?" Have him or her listen to the cd on the way to work or some other place. If you choose to record more than five songs, be sure that your recorded voice is after the second or third song, to be sure they hear the message. Try to be there waiting at the destination with the engagement ring.

6. Write a book confessing your love to your companion and have it published. Have the question within the book or upon releasing of the book or have the engagement ring attached to a bookmark. If you wish, you can have the bookmark personalized.

7. Rent out a movie theater and have the message "Will you marry me?" on the screen.

8. Pay to have a message placed on a billboard. Drive your companion to the spot and point to the billboard and then ask, "Will you?"

9. Tell a bedtime story or write one and have it published. Personalize the story, tell how you first met, include a few romantic memories, and end the story with the lover asking, "Will you marry me." At this time, you will pull out the engagement ring and ask what he or she says.

10. During Christmas time, have at least three gift boxes that fit inside of each other. So when your companion opens the first box it will be empty, the second will be empty, and the third will contain the ring.

11. Write and compose and song for your companion, popping the question.

12. Breakfast, lunch or dinner make a meal for companion, get down on knees, and ask question. You could make heart - shaped pancakes or any other desert of your choice.

13. In conversation Invite some friends over and have the dialog planned. Make sure that they continually say that you have something to ask, and then you finally agree and pop the question.

14. Dramatic play Get with director and have the actors say a line for you asking your companion to marry you for example, they may say, "Jill Smith, will you marry Jack Jones?" At this time make the engagement ring visible and get a confirmation.

15. Invite your companion to your church and talk with pastor about timing. Ask in front of congregation. It can be done in the form of a testimony. Or if possible, you can have the pastor include it in his morning message.

Short Stories

MEANT TO BE

"Dream big, kid, touch the sky," were the last spoken words of my favorite high school teacher right before graduation. I took those words to heart. It was no problem for me to dream big because I already was a dreamer and had always set high goals.

I was my own worst critic and therefore pushed myself very hard to achieve success. But of all of the dreams I had dreamed, I dreamed most about true love. I often wondered why my life couldn't be like my dreams.

I spent most of my time thinking about the perfect girl. Though I had been told I was attractive, I didn't take advantage of the opportunities to have a girlfriend. I had an idea of the perfect girl and no one measured up. I had the opportunity to date any girl I desired, but I wasn't interested. Therefore, my friends questioned my motives for not having a girlfriend. "Is he scared," they thought or " Is he gay?" However, these options were ruled out because my friends knew that I was too outgoing to be shy or scared. They also knew I wasn't gay. According to them, I didn't "act" gay whatever that is supposed to mean. I'd dated tons of girls, but I never had a true girlfriend, so most of the relationships were more like friendships. So, what was the problem, my friends often wondered. The problem was I could not find her, the one, my soul mate, my dream girl.

It was now fifteen years after high school and I was very accomplished. I had a six-figure salary, owned a beautiful four bedroom two and half bath house and an art gallery. But somehow my life seemed empty. My dreams seemed more fulfilling than my life.

Maybe this is why I enjoyed sleeping so much. But of all the dreams that I had, there was one that haunted me. I would have this dream night after night, no matter what else I had dreamed. It is about this beautiful woman dressed in white a white vision. She was so beautiful. She couldn't be real, but oh, how I wished she were. She had to be an illusion.

It would always begin with her singing Mariah Carey's "All I Want for Christmas," and she would come inside the door with a handful of gifts. I have always assumed it was Christmas, but I had dreamed this before Christmas.

"I," she would begin singing and then hand out the first gift. "...don't want a lot for Christmas / There is just one thing I need," she'd continue and pass out more gifts to the guests. "I don't care about the presents underneath the Christmas tree." Her voice is angelic and pure. She uplifts me as she sings. I've always thought singing was a way to celebrate, but what was being celebrated in this dream? I believed it to be a celebration of the day I meet my true love. In the dream, I just stare in admiration as she comes closer to me. "I just want you for my own / More than you would ever know / Make my wish come true," she sang.

By this time, she is directly in front of me. She bent down and sang the last words of the intro: "All I want for Christmas is you."

She then gives me a present. This is the part where I would always awake. Whenever I woke, I could still see her angelic face, her olive skin and silky jet-black curly hair. I had since been trying to interpret this dream. Was someone going to give me a gift? I'd come to the conclusion that maybe all she wants for Christmas was love and I was the personification of love. Whatever it meant, I hoped I found out instead of dreaming of it every night.

I was so intrigued by the woman in my dream that I created an oil painting of her and hung it in my home. I didn't show it to many people because I kept it in my study. The only person that has seen the painting is my friend Darrin. He is the only one I trust enough to tell about the inspiration for the painting. His reaction upon first seeing it was thinking I had finally gotten into a serious relationship. When I told him that the painting had been inspired by a recurring dream, he thought I was crazy. I would have to agree. It did feel strange having a connection to someone I've never met before, especially someone who wasn't even real.

I felt an eerie connection with the woman; as if she was near me, as if she was real. However, I knew she didn't exist. I had never seen her before or anyone who even looked similar.

Every night I would pray I would some day meet her. If I did, deep down inside, I knew she was the one. my phone rang. I turned over, disappointed that my dream had been interrupted.

"Hello."

"Hey, Chris. Man, wake up. I know you're still sleeping".

It was Darrin, whom I'd met when I first moved in town. We worked at the same art gallery until I decided to develop my own. He helped me get acquainted with the city and now we were business partners. It was 6:45 A.M. on a cold Christmas morning.

The windows were fogged, and the floor beneath me was freezing. Only Darrin would call me at this hour for no apparent reason other than to get on my nerves.

"Yeah, man, I was sleeping and having a good dream too."

"About your mystery lady," he joked.

"No", I lied. Sometimes I lied whenever Darrin would joke with me about the dream. I felt a bit strange having the same dream over and over again.

"If I were you," he continued, "I would dream about her too. After all, she is fine," he said, laughing.

"Very funny," I smiled. "What do you want at this hour."

"I was going to Atlanta with Tyah. I'm nervous; I'm going to meet her family for the first time."

"And?"

"I wanted to know if you wanted to come with us."

"Oh, I don't know," I groaned. Tyah was Darrin's girlfriend. They had been steady for quite some time now. I thought he might pop the question soon. Whenever they'd go somewhere, I would always be the third wheel. I didn't feel quite like being a spare at the moment. After all, I didn't know if I could endure all of the *lubby dubby* every two seconds.

"Oh come on, man. It's going to be fun," he begged. I could hear the desperation in his voice. "After all, you aren't doing anything else. Besides, I hear that Tyah's got some nice- looking friends. Come on. Please."

I had no choice but to give in at this point. I must admit that Darrin had been a good friend and had never let me down. If going with him on this trip would comfort his nerves, I was all for it. I wanted him to make a good impression on his future in-laws.

"Alright, alright, I'll go. What time do you want me to be ready?"

"In thirty minutes. Tyah and I are leaving now.

"Thirty minutes," I complained, not sure if I could be ready that soon.

"Yes, thirty minutes," he confirmed. "Bye."

Darin hung up the phone and was on his way. I dragged myself out of bed, groomed myself, and waited for Darrin. I slipped on an ivory pullover sweater and some khaki pants. I didn't feel like I looked my best, but this would have to do for now.

I heard the car horn; he and Tyah had arrived. I ran downstairs and threw my bag into the trunk. The entire ride there, I thought *What have I gotten myself into?*

We arrived in Atlanta about seven hours later. I met and greeted an onslaught of strangers. After about four hours of boredom and observing everyone else open gifts and enjoy their day, I heard someone unlocking the front door. When the door finally opened, the unbelievable happened. I saw a leg step in with a long, white, high-heeled boot. When the rest of the body slipped into the door, she was dressed in white jeans, a white trench coat, a white turtleneck underneath and a white Santa Clause cap. My mouth dropped open as she began doing the unthinkable. She began singing Mariah Carey's, "All I Want for Christmas."

For a moment, I thought that I was back at home in my bedroom dreaming. Strangely, I was not. Just as I had dreamed, she was directly in front of me when she said, "All I want for Christmas is you." However, instead of handing me a present, she hunched her shoulders up and smiled at me as she realized that she didn't have anymore presents.

She then bent down and gave me something better than any of the gifts that had been in the bag. She bent down, placed her hands in mine, and planted a kiss on my lower left cheek. In doing so, she slightly grazed my lips.

All of the attention was now on us as everyone in the room noticed the attraction we shared. But no one understood why.

Then I looked over and observed that Darrin's mouth had dropped open as he too was shocked at what had just happened. He recognized her all-too-familiar face and could not believe she was there in the same room. It was her; the woman in my dreams, the woman who I'd envisioned many nights and who covers the wall of my study.

"Hi, I'm Miko, Tiyah's cousin," she said, her voice even sweeter than I had ever dreamed. "I do this every year. I buy general gifts and give them to friends and family members. I guess I wasn't prepared this time."

"Wow," I responded, still surprised I was graced by the presence of an angel. "I can't believe this," I said as I stood to my feet. "It's nice to finally meet you, Miko."

"You must be Darrin," she said, because only Darrin was expecting to meet her. She'd assumed that Tyah had told Darrin about her. "My cousin has told me so much about you. It's nice to finally meet you too."

I just smiled as I stared into her eyes. "I'm Chris, Darrin's friend. I traveled here with him and Tyah."

"Were you expecting to meet me?" she asked curiously.

"No, but I'm glad that I finally have. You look just as I imagined," I said still staring at her in amazement. She must have thought that I was some sort of psycho.

"Do we know each other?" She grew even more curious.

"Somewhat," I said with a sly smile, afraid to tell her how I knew of her. This would only confirm her thoughts.

"How so?" she asked

"You wouldn't believe me if I told you. But I have a feeling you will learn."

"I need to get dinner started," she said and invited me into the kitchen.

I walked with her into the kitchen and she asked, "What do you do for a living?"

"I am an artist; I own an art gallery."

"That's great! I love art," she said with excitement. "I've actually always wanted a portrait painted of myself. How much would you charge me for something like that and how long does it usually take?"

I just smiled and said,"Miko, that won't be a problem. Consider your portrait already complete."

"So, what is it that I won't believe if you told me?"

This question caught me off guard. I didn't know how she'd react if I told her that I had a picture of her hanging in my study.

So, I just smiled and scratched my head. My only response was, "I will tell you one day, but I don't think you're ready."

"You'll be surprised what I'd believe. After all, I've had my share of strange occurrences."

"Maybe, but not as strange as what I have encountered."

"Would you feel more comfortable if I shared mine first?" she asked trying to pry my secret out of me.

"I don't know. But if you'd like to share, go ahead. Meanwhile, I'll think about sharing my story."

"All right," she smiled slyly. "Come here," she said as she took my hand and invited me to follow her.

I followed her into a back room, but I did not expect what was to come next. When she opened the door, my heart began pacing, my blood ran cold, and my mouth could not stay shut. There upon the wall behind the neatly made bed was a painting of me. My right hand was extended with a white rose, and I was wearing a white tuxedo in the painting.

"I'm an artist too," she finally revealed. "My drawings are inspired by my dreams. This one was inspired by a recurring dream of the man that I dreamed to marry."

At that point, my heart sank and I cuffed her left cheek with my right hand and said, "So you dreamed of me too; this was meant to be."

The Blessing

Today was no ordinary day, for me, and last night was no ordinary night. I had gotten only three hours of sleep. I tossed and turned, walked and jogged throughout my house last night. I guess this is what happens to a brave man stricken by love. Her name is Marie Sanders. We had been going steady for about a year now, and she was every man's dream. She was angelically beautiful, intelligent, fun, charismatic, and most importantly a devout Christian. Beauty wasn't everything; what made her even more beautiful was her love of the Lord. We had first met in church; during which time I was in the market for a new church home. I attended Holiness Missionary Baptist Church. It was composed mostly of elderly members and quite frankly the service had grown boring. I had been a member since I was a child. Now that I was a man, I wanted to choose my own church. At that point in my life, I was looking for more out of church. I was looking for a church that made a joyful noise in honor of God; a church that wasn't afraid to change with the times a little. Holiness Missionary was filled with people who sat in service with their nice suits and high hats, too afraid to dance for the Lord. We sang mostly the same songs and the pastor disapproved of music by Kirk Franklin, praise dances, and women pastors.

As for me, it was time for a change. My friend Mark had told me about his church, House of God, and advised me I would enjoy the service. Mark had been my friend since the seventh grade and has never steered me in the wrong direction. In school we were known as "double trouble," since my name was Mark too. I took his advice and visited one Sunday. He was right; I did enjoy myself. The music was great and the congregation surely knew how to praise the Lord. This was my type of crowd.

Then I saw something I wasn't used to seeing at Holiness Missionary or any other church I had visited. I saw a beautiful young woman shouting for the Lord. She appeared to be no older than twenty -one. I noticed her in the pews on my right praising God like there was no tomorrow. She was full of energy. She danced and shouted through most of the service.

At the end of the service, I was finally able to meet her and get a good look at her face. She was ethereal. She was dressed in a lavender, two-piece skirt set and a ravishing lavender hat. At first, I could only see the rim of the hat until she held up her head.

She extended her right arm and shook my hand. I felt the power emanating from her. If this life was heaven, she was surely the pearly gates.

"Hi, I'm Sister Marie Sanders," she said as she extended her hand and smiled. "It's nice to meet you."

"I'm Mark Allen," I said, trembling inside, overwhelmed by her presence. "I'm visiting from Holiness Missionary Baptist Church. I'm here with my friend, Mark Suthers."

"Well, we certainly are glad to have you here at House of God. Please, come again," she requested.

Her request was granted as I continued to visit every Sunday after before I decided to finally join the church. Marie and I became friends and eventually love interests. We would spend our spare time at revivals, quiet picnics, restaurants, and on the beach. We had some great times together and I wanted to do this forever. Matter of fact, I wanted to ask her to marry me. This is what had kept me up all night. I was worried sick. I thought: Would she have me? Was she ready? Was this even the right time? I didn't have the answer to any of these questions but was hoping that the answer would appear somewhere. I was in bad shape. I prayed for a sign from heaven. I needed reassurance whether this was the right time.

I stopped the guess work and put on my beige Armani suit, gold cufflinks, and beige and brown Stacy Adams shoes. I prayed the entire way to church. Marie and I had planned to meet at church and have dinner following the service. I had planned on popping the question during dinner. But I wanted something special for Marie; I wanted the proposal to be memorable. However, I was unable to come up with a great way to accomplish this.

I went and prayed during the alter call and again asked God for a sign. Reverend Nixon began preaching. He had gotten half way through another meaningful sermon yet I hadn't heard a word. I asked for the Lord's forgiveness as I was not paying attention.

I was worried about my situation until Reverend Nixon's voice rose and he quoted a line from Corinthians 7:9, "For is better to marry than burn."

This is it, I thought. This was my sign; it was meant for me to marry Marie. I felt as if he was preaching this sermon just for me. At this point, my adrenaline rushed and I stood to my feet.

"Reverend, Reverend," I interrupted. "You speak the truth. Love is beautiful and it is through God that we love one another.

As God created us, he created one for us to love, and Sister Marie Saunders is the one for me. We have been Christian friends for quite sometime, and today, I'm asking her to be my wife. We first met right here in church and I can think of no place better to ask for her hand in marriage than in the house of the Lord. We shall also be united here...if she'll marry me".

I turned to Marie who was sitting next to me, and I pulled her into the aisle, got down on one knee, and asked her to marry me.

"Marie, will you marry me," I said with every muscle in my body trembling.

She just stood there looking as beautiful as ever. She smiled and flashed her beautiful teeth, which forced her dimples to show. Her eyes were glistening with tears of joy. I could see that she was shaking too. She placed one hand over her mouth and cried for a second and finally said, "In the name of the Father, in the name of the Son, and the Holy Spirit, yes! Yes! I will!

"Let the church say, Amen," said Reverend Nixon.

Everyone in the congregation stood to their feet and applauded us. Marie and I embraced each other.

"Thank you Jesus, thank you Jesus," I whispered as tears began streaming down my face and I squeezed her even tighter.

The Lord answered my prayers, Marie was truly a blessing.

About Author

Keri Brye is a high school English instructor and journalism advisor. She is also an achieved writer, poet, and journalist. She writes for the *New American Press*, an African American publication and has free lanced for the *Pensacola News Journal.* She attended Florida A and M University in Tallahassee. She lives in Pensacola, Florida, with her daughter and husband. For more information on upcoming books, visit her web site at http://keri- brye@tripod.com or if you have any comments, contact her at keri-brye@lycos.com

• • •

To all my readers,

Thank you for all of your support in purchasing this book. If you like what you have read and would like information on upcoming books, please contact me at keri-brye@lycos.com or on my website at http://www.keri-bryeon-line.net. Once again, thank you for all of your support, and I am always interested in your feedback.